Leading a Life

Georgia Ressmeyer

Water's Edge Press

Copyright © 2021 by Georgia Ressmeyer

All rights reserved.

Printed in the United States of America

Water's Edge Press LLC
Sheboygan, WI
watersedgepress.com

ISBN: 978-1-952526-06-0

Credits:

Cover photography by the author
Author photo by Dawn Hogue

With thanks to early readers of this book—especially Lois Torkelson, Marilyn Zelke-Windau, and Christa Klein—for their helpful suggestions and support.

A Water's Edge Press First Edition

"This little book is a gem. With warmth and affection, Ressmeyer sketches poignant stories that help to destigmatize mental illnesses and to affirm some of their quirky vulnerabilities common to us all. In nine engaging snapshots of troubled souls caught up by the Law for a variety of societal outlier behaviors, she reveals these women and men to be the funny, courageous, adaptive and resilient beings that they clearly are, in all their garbled and tender beauty. Her insightful exploration of their—and of her own—experiences of disjointed thought and unregulated mood change, of "shrieks of joy" and hope's "crash landing," and perhaps especially of "keeping weakness under wraps" can be welcomed by all readers open to the universal realities of simply leading a human life."

—Janet E. Tatman, PhD, PA-C Emeritus, Clinical Psychologist and Physician Assistant (retired), Fellow American Academy of Sleep Medicine/Certified in Behavioral Sleep Medicine

"Georgia Ressmeyer's poems are skillfully written, replete with satisfying sounds and techniques. Yet their real value is that they go beyond a capable craft. These pieces are eye-openers; they reveal a world most of us have never seen, but they also lead to introspection and self-realization. The poet copes with the weight of the past and a frenetic pace of life by encapsulating memories in familiar images that offer comfort in a dangerous world. The reader is not pulled down by despair but offered a dichotomy of anxiety and hope that ultimately heals."

— Jan Chronister, author of *Decennia* (Truth Serum Press)

"Georgia Ressmeyer takes us on a journey from the courtroom to a woman reflecting through the looking glass. Each poem provides historical memories with profound emotion. Her lyrics set the stage for owning our story and bringing forth inner peace. Ressmeyer demonstrates through words that compassion, empathy, and transparency can set us free."

—Julie L. Preder, Executive Director,
Mental Health America Sheboygan County

Also by Georgia Ressmeyer

Today I Threw My Watch Away
Waiting to Sail
Home/Body

Acknowledgements

The author is grateful to the editors of the following publications in which these poems first appeared, some in slightly different form:

Phantasmagoria: "I Have Consumed Enough"

South Carolina Review: "Lost Therapist"

The Museletter: "Isn't Everybody Manic Some of the Time?"

Wisconsin People & Ideas: "Her Statement"

Wisconsin Review: "The Queen of Pride"

Wisconsin Poets' Calendar 2019: Celebrating Wisconsin People: " Chaos Makes You Anxious"

Waiting to Sail (Black River Press, 2014): "Leading a Life," "Queen of the Courtroom," "Song for Two Voices," "The Human Mind," "Throwing Glue at the Police"

Home/Body (Pebblebrook Press: an Imprint of *Stoneboat*, 2017): "Addicted," "An American History," "Each Other's Keepers"

Dedication

For many years I worked as a defense lawyer in a large city. I met most of my clients for the first time at the county's mental health complex, where they were confined based on allegations of recent statements or behaviors that were believed to show they posed a danger to themselves or others.

In my job as a public defender, I spent countless hours talking with clients, reviewing medical charts, negotiating with doctors and county attorneys, and defending my clients in court. Most cases were either dismissed outright or settled by agreements to cooperate with treatment for a specified period of time.

The first part of this book contains sketches of encounters with clients that took place more than thirty-five years ago. These have been reconstructed from journal entries and disguised to protect privacy. Two are composites. The second part includes poems exploring depression, mania, addiction, anxiety, and living on the edge—states that often go undiagnosed in the general population, though they exist wherever human beings struggle to maintain balance.

For me the greatest reward for my work was getting to know the people I represented, whose resilience, unique perspectives on life and language, and gentle or pointed observations were the source of much of the joy I felt as an attorney. They enriched my existence and inspired this book, which I dedicate to them with gratitude.

Leading a Life

Throwing Glue at the Police 1
Queen of the Courtroom 2
John Doe, Hero 4
Her Statement 5
An American History 6
A Silent Declaration 8
Each Other's Keepers 10
Leading a Life 12
Mystified 14

Wayward Thoughts

The Human Mind 19
Isn't Everybody Manic Some of the Time? 20
Wayward Thoughts 21
I Have Consumed Enough 22
The Queen of Pride 23
Stress 24
Addicted 25
A Moment's Peace 26
The Argument 27
Hope Dips 28
Lost Therapist 29
Chaos Makes You Anxious 30
Sing a String 31
Magic Pill 32
Song For Two Voices 33

"In illness words seem to possess a mystic quality. We grasp what is beyond their surface meaning, gather instinctively this, that, and the other – a sound, a colour, here a stress, there a pause... In health meaning has encroached upon sound. Our intelligence domineers over our senses. But in illness, with the police off duty, ... the words give out their scent, and ripple like leaves, and chequer us with light and shadow, and then, if at last we grasp the meaning, it is all the richer for having travelled slowly up with all the bloom upon its wings."

Virginia Woolf
On Being Ill

Leading a Life

Throwing Glue at the Police

As we walked into the courtroom, my client
accosted her psychiatrist and said, pointing at me,
"This woman just accused me of throwing glue
at the police! I didn't throw no glue at the police!"

I took her aside and told her it was a shoe, not glue,
and that the police, not me, were the ones claiming
she'd flung it at them.

My client paced and mumbled, "Nobody goes
around throwing glue at the police in the alley."
To her, such an accusation was beyond the pale,
even crazy.

Suddenly she grabbed the paper we'd been discussing
and proceeded to sign herself into the hospital
for two weeks. Maybe she'd come to the conclusion
that conditions on the outside were a lot worse
than she'd imagined.

Since then, to my knowledge, no one has been detained
by the police for throwing glue at them in an alley—
though there were days, grueling days, when I
contemplated lurking in just such a byway with a tube
of adhesive, waiting for law enforcement to happen by
so I could fling some at their squad car, or at least
drop glue onto their shoes. I figured this might
slow them down, keep them from adding so many
new clients to my caseload.

Queen of the Courtroom

She was Queen of the Courtroom, dispensing
her bounty with grace and warmth. She glowed
and spread good cheer and compliments
like butter on a slice of just-baked bread.

Some smiled to see her slather up the room,
shaking everybody's hand, flattering them about
their teeth, their eyes, their obvious intelligence.
A few—the ones who knew her best—
returned her winks.

The nursing students sitting in on court—
blank-faced, thunderstruck—visibly shrank
in fear when she approached their group to say
how pleased she was that they could come.
She claimed to be "a modest woman," then
raised her hospital gown to show them bruises
on her upper thigh—inflicted, she said, by
two of the petitioners in the case.

During the hearing she interrupted every witness,
yelling "Lies!" "You're under oath!" or
"Tell the truth!" She tried to cross-examine
some of them herself, including the psychiatrist
who'd labeled her "bipolar" and "manic."
No one could silence her.

We lost the hearing, although my client never lost
the rapt attention of all present. Afterwards she
refused to leave the courtroom until she'd shaken
every willing hand, wished all a happy holiday,
and told a few how beautiful they were.

For the court commissioner who ruled against her she had a different message. Shaking that reluctant hand, my client said, "I do a lot for humanity."

And so she did—especially for those of us in thankless jobs who occasionally enjoyed our court hearings sunny-side up and our rare praises laid on thick by the Queen of the Courtroom whenever she deigned to favor us with her presence.

John Doe, Hero

He was young and thin when I met him,
had pins in both legs from a suicide
attempt, wore glasses and a moustache,
whined a lot.

One day another male patient pinned
a nurse on the floor, was about to
stab her with a dinner fork when my
client flung his body at the attacker and
held him till staff could intervene.

After the incident he became "John Doe,
Hero"—so named by the press in news
accounts. Staff treated him with more
respect, he grew happier with himself,
and best of all, he stopped whining.

No one was more shocked by his quick,
courageous act than he was. "I just
had to do it," he told me later, shaking
his head in wonder.

"I'm proud of you," I said. Moments later
he offered me all his money. I reminded
him that he'd never regain control of his own
finances if he kept giving everything away.

I like to think that now, all these years
later, he's living in his own house, paying
his bills on time, and occasionally
recounting the story of his past heroic act.

A few of us—including the nurse whose
neck he saved—will never need reminding.

Her Statement

Yesterday morning I'm pretty sure it was yesterday
I started walking along the beach toward someone who
would meet me at my destination. Where it was or
who it was I can't remember off the top of my head.

I walked that way a hundred times before and knew
my feet would take the right path through the woods
when the rocks became too high to climb.

Near some bushes that leaned into the path I sat down
to tie my shoe. Then I saw wild raspberries growing
over my head and ate a few. They tasted so much like
lunch that I figured this must be my destination
and stayed for a long time eating and waiting.

Then night came and I heard boys shouting, laughing
and cursing as they climbed the rocks. I could tell
they were not for me so I curled up and slept
on the overgrown path.

There were rustlings in the woods all around me
and once a soft tail or whisker brushed my cheek
but no one came to meet me.

In the morning I crawled back out to the beach and
sat there on a pile of rocks to watch the sun come up.
I could see its heart beating in the shimmer of its giant
orange eye. My own eyes beat in time with it and
somewhat cried.

Later a woman came and said she would walk me to
the street which she did and then I went up and down
each one until I found a house that fit the key on the ledge
at the top of the door. I came inside and I was here.
And that is everything I know about what happened.

An American History

She was never actually a client, never the subject
of an active case, just a woman who was housed,
more than thirty years ago, on the top floor
of the mental health center in long-term care,
having no hope or expectation of getting out—
possibly an angel, I thought, who had lost her way.

She was early middle-aged, slightly plump, always
wore a dress, had brown hair that was thinning
somewhat—probably a side-effect of all the
medications she was required to take.

The first time she called my office, it was to ask
if I could please make the hospital stop forcing her
to have so many babies. She'd already given birth
22,000 times—which, she said, was exhausting.

Later she called to say that the hospital had removed
part of her brain—"the happiness memories of
my childhood"—and could I please find a surgeon
who would put them back.

She told me she'd recently seen a little girl
in the canteen whom she knew to be her own.
"We have the same eyebrows," she said.
"Normally when I'm with children my voice
goes into the high registers, but today I was like
a little, dead leaf."

Once she invited me into her room to show me
her "Christmas Card to the World," signed
with her full name and displayed on her dresser
year-round.

She let me look at her books, which included
War and Peace and a novel by Henry James—
though she hadn't been able to finish these—
a Bible, a book about the Bible, and a history book.
"I really like to read books about the American
history," she said.

Another time she called and told me, "Some
people think I'm the Virgin Mary. I don't know
if it's true, but Joseph of Bethlehem says I look
like her. I'm trying to marry Joseph of Bethlehem,
except I don't know whether he's going to
come through for me or not."

Although I never did find a surgeon who could put
the "happiness memories" of childhood back
in her brain, she was always gracious to me, and
grateful for any attention I paid her.

Years later, the top-floor, long-term care units
were emptied out and their residents moved to
community placements. I picture my non-client
residing contentedly among her books and other
precious possessions in a group home or apartment.

But who knows: maybe Joseph finally came
through with a proposal. Maybe the two are
happily married and living in Bethlehem, with
babies she's allowed to keep.

A Silent Declaration

Her arms hugging her chest,
eyes downcast, no wish to talk,
nothing to say, no one to trust.

A hospital bathrobe as good
a costume as any she could wear.
A doorjamb to lean on in lieu of
a chair. Food becoming irrelevant.

I learned from others that she
graduated from college, worked
at a halfway house in a distant city,
returned home uncommunicative,
angry with the father she'd once
adored. Depression ran in the family.

Our conversation was short. She
made eye-contact with me twice,
probably to see if she could trust me.

Her eyes were mournful, probing,
far from the rushed, goal-oriented
world I tried to keep from flooding
out of mine.

After I explained her legal options,
she rasped, "Dismiss." On her behalf
I went to court—she declined to join me—
and won a dismissal on technical grounds.

Her father was incensed, harangued
the court commissioner, shook his fist,
threatened to sue her for incompetence.

In the meantime my client signed herself
into the hospital voluntarily, uncoerced
by her parents, the court, anyone else.

She accepted treatment, was discharged
soon after, became involved in a church
serving homeless people, got married,
gave birth. I lost touch with her after that.

These days I wonder if she's still
a woman of few words, and what she
talks about when she does speak.

Each Other's Keepers

He was tormented when I met him: snakes everywhere,
electrocutions, explosions, dark circles under his eyes,
pants falling down, hadn't eaten in days, tried to
suffocate his mother with one hand—or so the police
claimed—though he said he'd been trying to protect her
from breathing poisonous fumes.

When we sat down to discuss the commitment case
against him he asked, "What would you do if you went
down to the basement of your house and you saw
that three people were trapped in the furnace with
a boa constrictor and none of them had eaten in a week?"

He said there were bombs going off all around him,
exploding under his feet. He could hear the explosions
a second apart. I asked whether the sounds he heard
might possibly be the beat of his own heart. "No,"
he said, without anger, pointing at the floor, "it's
coming from down there."

He told me he had three big worries about staying
at the hospital: his dog, who required medical attention;
his mother, who was old and weak and needed him
around the house; and the people in the furnace,
who had to be gotten out.

At his request we telephoned his mother. She was
elated to hear he was accepting medication. She
asked if he would have to stay in the hospital long.
"I'm an old woman," she said, "and frail. It's hard
for me to get along without him."

Later that day his mother called and told me he was
fine when he took meds. "He cooks for himself,"
she said, "takes out the garbage, puts my storm
windows up. I do his laundry but he pays me for that."
Then she added, "All we have is each other.
There's no one else to talk to."

How long did she live, I wonder, and what happened
to him after she was gone?

I don't worry about her. She obviously had a gift for
adapting with good grace to whatever the future brought.
Her son, I believe, inherited a portion of that.

Leading a Life

It's 1984. A client at the mental health center
tells me she's wired to a telephone pole
behind her house, and that her movements are
transmitted on TV for purposes of "dirty sex."
She can't leave until those wires are cut.

She's sure it's still her house even without
utilities, despite what the city claims, how often
they condemn it, or how many padlocks
they put on the doors.

Once those wires are cut, she says, the city can
take her house—if they still want it—and she
can lead a normal life. "I know how to lead
a life," she adds. "I'm not 'mental.'"

She denies owing past-due property taxes,
says "No one pays taxes these days,"
and "No one uses money."

She tells me she's eighty-five, then tells
someone else she's fifty. I ask her why she
does this. She smiles and says, "You have to
tell them something."

The house is the house she grew up in,
a bungalow west of the river,
in the neighborhood where I live, too.

Of course she's wired to that house—
couldn't not be after so many years spent in one
familiar place amid the odors and shimmering
forms of family, all now deceased.

It's her house and will remain so—until
Death with his wire-cutters comes to make that
final cut, as he did for her parents and siblings.

I convince the court to dismiss the commitment
case against her, which had been initiated
by the city to ease the seizing of her home.

Then I find a legal services attorney to help her
get it back. I give her a winter coat and boots I don't
wear much, and drive her to a homeless shelter,
hoping she'll accept services and stay put for a while.

On my way back to the office I wonder if, when
I reach her age, I'll be as wily and resilient and
loyal to my memories and to my house
as she is to hers—

or will I one day go to meet a client on the wards
and, forgetting to bring my briefcase, be so
indistinguishable from most patients that staff
won't let me leave, and will I be relieved and not
protest, and will I take whatever meds I'm told
are best?

Mystified

1. Client

Rosalind throws out her shoes   God tells her to
    she says   to prove her trust:
         in what   *in what*
  Step off the curb in traffic   nude

I pray that God   or some kind mortal
  will do the saving work   her faith expects:
    catch   halfway-to-the-gutter feet
    lift   soles over cars
      plant   safely on the other side
  of what   *of what*

She resonates to sacred music   bends a knee to
    statues   altars   crosses

Hers is just a simple cross   of street
  no Middle Passage   Delaware   or Calvary
    An ordinary act   dozens of times a week

She comes to pray   and
    haloes embrace her   auras   echoes
      trances   whispers   voices

She believes in Miracles   Forgiveness of sins   Life
  Everlasting   and   it all makes sense

She's sure no harm can come   when   she bathes
    in the bloodied fountains of
Jesus' cupped hands   or curls for shelter under
    the oozing arches of Jesus' feet
        cold   concrete   night
        after shuddering
  night   after shuddering   night

2. Public Defender

I come to pray   and
        doubts betray me   murmurs
    curses   groans   I'm not alone
        never alone   never not two
            ears for   undertone

The mystery of misery I flee from   reading
        tucked in my briefcase
    rage and loss   I hear
    rebukes each place I go   I keep
            my back bent   eyes turned
                            low

Who is the Defender   who the Client
    who's the sane one   who   isn't
    who's the judge of Faith   or Reason
        who locks the doors   who
                    tries to pick them

I'm with the Mystified   knowing
        and not knowing the going rate
    for Truth   I'd rather drug
        myself   than lose that rite
            to doctors   or to Court

I freely pop myself a beer   or cork
        distract myself   with hollow joys
                with noise   more
            noise   until I'm numb

I pray no harm will come to those   who bathe
        in the bloodied fountains of
Jesus' cupped hands   or curl for shelter under
          the oozing arches of Jesus' feet
               cold   concrete   night
                     after shuddering
    night   after shuddering   night

Wayward Thoughts

The Human Mind

How fragile the human mind is:
watermelon gone splat from a flatbed truck
      seeds of thought caught in the treads
            of tires speeding away

What skull can contain the whole
      keep safe sane warm all sense
of what anything means when rattled
      like a baby's toy by passersby
            babbling sounds but
                  brooking no responses

a flock of starlings buzzing whistling
      in throngs on fields of grass
            like fleas on cats
                  distractions to
                        disheveled hosts

a knotted mass of sewing-basket debris
      working itself free from the points
            and jabs of endless
                  repetitive intrusions
huddled now in soft repose
            with other tangled fuses

Isn't Everybody Manic Some of the Time?

My inflated beach-ball brain scuds across
the water on a burst of thought.

The speed of transport exhilarates me.
Bouncing unleashes shrieks of joy.

Who's that swimmer-after, that headless
body flailing to catch up?

Faster, wind, if you're promoting freedom.
My pursuer is a tyrant.

Rotate my colors, spin me like a pinwheel
as I leap from wave to wave.

Instead the wind abruptly holds its breath,
dropping me to a sit-still.

Hands reach out and seize, squeezing too
hard, pressing the air out of my bliss.

They level all my best. Who am I now?
A plastic pancake stuffed in a beach bag.

Wayward Thoughts

In the sieve of my brain my thoughts
are washed. The dregs of some
are filtered out. Only the tiny grains
squeeze through.

So flighty now, so fine, they dance
like sand, they roll and wheel to wind
and whimsy only they are able
to detect.

I find I cannot mold grains into sense.
They won't stay put, keep drifting off,
side-stepping my unwavering intent
to line them up.

Don't hold us back, their actions say.
Don't herd us into rows.
We're meant for greater things,
like rolling with waves.

New efforts to restrain and organize
these tiny thoughts stay futile.
Their wills are stronger than their
flimsy forms suggest.

At last I quit promoting sense they
find nonsensical, too limiting—
and which, they say, no bright
ideas can dance to!

I Have Consumed Enough

I wake to unresilience,
prayers not answered.

Mind hobbles,
hallways seem endless.

Marbles lurk underfoot
to unbalance walks,
indignitize momentum.

I live for sleep,
cocooning in my naps.

Hope is this pupal state
from which
on coming wings
my soul projects escape.

I have no need to dress
or eat or move my feet.

The Queen of Pride

Please do not ask the Queen of Pride to go
unmediated through the world. She needs
a crutch, one that is slender as a reed
if not invisible. No one must know
the price she paid for it—too high, too low,
or that she paid a price at all. Her creed
of keeping weakness under wraps now leads
to such dissemblance that her fear just grows
that she will be unmasked, the brace kicked out
from under her. She dare not show her dread
of being made a fool, nor can she shout
or call attention to herself. The bed
this Queen has made, on which she now must lie,
has needles in it, but she will not cry.

Stress

You're in a rush. Your brain jumps
side to side, forward, back,
hops in multiple dimensions.

The mind in charge is too charged up
to give directions. You'd settle for
suggestions, a progression of steps
leading to a goal, however slight—
washing dishes, for example.

The skills for doing simple tasks
are present, but no one prioritizes,
propels your limbs in useful patterns.

You're as scattered as the pieces
of a jigsaw puzzle pounced on
by a jealous cat. You'd better lock
that feline, briefly, in the kitchen,
give yourself a chance.

Then find and snap the interlocking
bits in place, create an image
that makes sense—a rocky shoreline,
for example.

Maybe that will give you confidence
to do as much with all the messes
you face. Of course, there's always
a chance this will add to your stress,
but you're used to that.

Stress pulls the puppet strings that
keep you on your feet, frenetically
engaged with life, whether you're
accomplishing or not.

Addicted

To be transported to a better place
to an altered state we drink alcohol
eat cake meditate smoke tobacco or
weed have sex binge on chocolate
sip cappuccino fall in love drive too fast
gormandize pop a pill guzzle soda
inject heroin read books play games
watch movies text incessantly
exercise too much sleep too little
write poems listen to music sing songs
dance till dawn get high on our own
natural chemical imbalances — Who's
to say what is and isn't an acceptable trip
when we're all addicted to something
or someone and most get away with it?

A Moment's Peace

The head I hold in my hands is mine,
cheekbones snug on the pads of my palms,
eyes and eyebrows calm in their flesh-lined tents,
forehead soothed by cool-feeling fingers.

I could be any age, belong to any:
crouched by a fire in a cave at night,
a refugee in a crowded camp,
my father at ninety, not hungry,
waiting for Mom to stop stabbing at her mouth
with a spoon that shakes,
life winding down, closing off the world
for a few seconds' peace, prayerful or blank,
cradling bones and flesh in bones and flesh —

until I'm called back to the world of want:
free Dad's walker from the stack,
remove Mom's bib and guide her in her wheelchair
out of the room through a hedge of legs.

I miss the days, not long ago, when
both my parents were still fully present.

Now I am bereft even when I'm with them:
Dad cocooned in sleep,
Mom staring past me at shapes I cannot see,
shining her soul to meet them.

The Argument

The storm: east wind, a rage of waves,
wet snow that melted at first
but later stuck
like words of insult piling up
against shifting rocks, a defenseless,
indefensible shore,
gangs of truths, half-truths, lies,
assumptions, some accurate,
many just imagined,
waves hurled that could not be recoiled
and gently tucked into the beds
from which they'd sprung,
no threat to physical safety but
smarting, like beads of sleet stinging
cheeks, matting eyelashes or glasses,
distorting vision,
making every step of eastbound
confrontation a descent into
confusion, a loss of self and place
from which reversing course—
retreating, yes avoiding—
seemed the only safe choice
and so I turned, fled home
and tried to get warm
recalling shrieked words that
still flared into flame in my throat.

Hope Dips

Hope dips, a wind-abandoned
kite that can't be saved by
tugging on its string, and dives
and will not try to save itself
and will not rise, not envy
dragonflies or pray for wings.

Hope's landing is a crash, with
splintering. No one regrets the
passing of a passive thing. It
lies unmourned, a tattered bit
of stuff that would not fly, not
will itself onto a higher plane,

not miss the waning of birds'
songs, the energy with which they
strung their nests. Late summer
settles back and drifts, as hope
drifts and shuts its eyes and falls,
not sensing that it falls, and dies.

Lost Therapist

In shrouded halls I feel along the walls for doors
and find a tantalizing knob that opens like a scab
into the anteroom of long-forgotten gouges.

A row of crimson couches lines this space
where I lie down and wait for healing thoughts
to lance or lace me up for further tries

at squeezing through invisible defenses. "Where
might I find an exit?" I ask politely, though my
words now dangle above my head as a reproach.

Must seek that door myself, must keep on
fumbling in the smoke. No one will come to lead
me out. I am, it seems, my own lost therapist.

Chaos Makes You Anxious

—and here she is,
ribbons and bundles flapping,
gnats in her tangle of hair.

You reach out to help her stand,
swat at her rags, her halo
of wires and threads.

You call her Peace,
which she's not. You hug her
to stop the commotion.

You dance a slow dance.
You ask if she remembers
how, years ago, the two

of you sometimes leaned
your heads together
for comfort and calm.

She's convinced you're wrong
but plays along, says,
"I was a mossy rock, too."

Sing a String

of haywire thoughts, balance
lost, sleep done without,
pain, elation, desperation.

Tell yourself you're only human,
can't be as constant as a tree.
Your mind rebels, it bellows

for relief. Sing words off-key,
randomly, nonsensically —
LOUDLY if that helps.

Don't be inhibited by any audience.
The only consciousness you
need to pierce is yours.

Others may try to shut you up.
Do not stop singing even if they
turn the microphone off.

This moment—now—is your
eternity, your timeless channel
to Justice and Truth.

The help you seek is in your voice—
so shriek! The words will come.
Listen to yourself!

Magic Pill

The magic pill you swallow
is not the one to save you,
though it will draw you back
into the mouthpiece of the wind's
tin trumpet, where silence is. All
soundlessness begins with you.

Where will you go, not groaning?
Will you kazoo? Will you blow
bubbles through a straw?

Death's not for you, the end of
breath not yet. As long as winter
won't let up, you're stuck in its
merciless surf, sucked out, flung
back.

Winter lives your life and does
the busywork you can't. Lie back
and let it die a drawn-out death.
After that, reset yourself in peace:
kazoos, some tulips, sweet rebirth.

Song For Two Voices

What if the day comes
        loudly like a robin's passion song

when nothing's left for me but
        Spring with fringe on all her limbs

empty corridors, empty rooms
        grown through every crack she finds

without a chair for resting on
        weaves nests below the overhang

shuffling lost from box to box
        draws flowers out of every stalk

not knowing when or if I can
        gives birth to countless living things

locate a door to exit from
        explodes in color, globes of light

www.ingramcontent.com/pod-product-compliance
Lightning Source LLC
Chambersburg PA
CBHW072040060426
42449CB00010BA/2378